Ï1

Th

brightly at Ripon for over 1300 years. The first church on this site was built by St Wilfrid in the 7th century. Wilfrid's Crypt still lies peacefully preserved beneath the later grandeur of the medieval Minster. But most of what you will see dates back to the 12th century. Today, Ripon Cathedral serves as the Mother Church of the Diocese of Ripon and Leeds. This is why it is called a cathedral – the church where you find the bishop's throne (cathedra in Latin). It is a place of worship and prayer, and home to a vibrant Christian community. As you walk around, you will see reflections of its many identities throughout the ages as a monastery, minster, shrine, and cathedral church. Ripon Cathedral is a working cathedral which serves the needs of the diocese. Unusually, it is also a parish church serving the local community. The Chapter (or governing body) is also responsible for maintaining traditions of choral excellence, and preserving a remarkable building for future generations. We welcome worshippers, pilgrims, and visitors alike to this ancient and holy place.

THE NAVE

The nave [1] was the centre of parish life in the Middle Ages, and was originally built by Archbishop Roger de Pont l'Evêque in the Transitional style during the 12th century (see p.24). Fragments of Roger's work can still be seen at the extreme east and west of both nave arcades [2]. In 1450, the central tower collapsed, necessitating a lengthy period of reconstruction. The nave was rebuilt with side aisles and a clerestory between 1502 and 1515. The work was probably overseen by Christopher Scune, who also worked on Durham Cathedral. If you walk down the side aisles [3] and look up at where the walls meet the vaults, you will see the coats of arms of the benefactors. In the south aisle are those of Archbishop Thomas Savage (1501-1507), and the Pigot family, while in the north aisle those of Cardinal Archbishop Christopher Bainbridge (1508-1514) and Fountains Abbey. The wooden ceiling of the main body of the nave is based on the medieval transept ceilings of York Minster and was erected by Sir George Gilbert Scott in the 1860s.

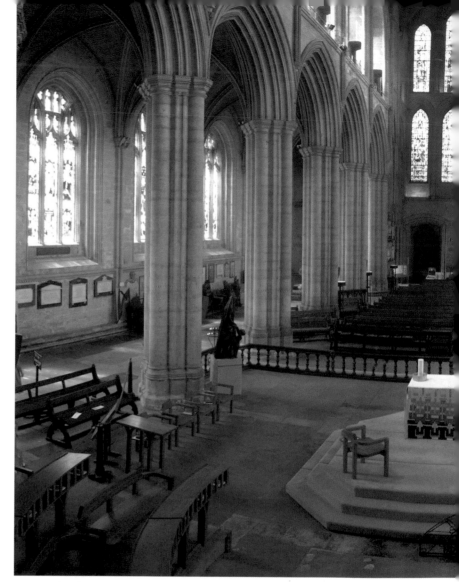

The 16th-century Frosterley marble font [4] is still used for the baptism of children and adults almost every Sunday.

This medieval tomb chest [6] is covered with a marble slab, into which is incised a man kneeling beside a lion in a grove of trees. It is probably the work of a 14th-century Flemish workshop.

The wall monument to Hugh Ripley [8], last Wakeman and first Mayor of Ripon (d. 1637), was restored in the 18th century following damage during the Civil War.

The nave [1] incorporates building work from the 12th, 13th, and 16th centuries. It has always been the most public part of the church and its altar continues to be the focus of parish worship.

This roundel of late 13th-century glass shows St Peter holding the keys to the Kingdom of Heaven. It is one of a number of roundels of medieval glass from the east window of the chancel now preserved at the west end of the south nave aisle [5].

The copper and marble Arts and Crafts pulpit [7] was made in 1913 by Henry Wilson. The four bronze figures represent the Anglo-Saxon saints Cuthbert, Chad, Hild, and Etheldreda.

THE CRYPT

The entrance to Wilfrid's Crypt [9] is clearly marked behind the choir stalls on the south side of the nave. The crypt, constructed in 672 beneath the High Altar of Wilfrid's Church, consists of two vaulted chambers. It is linked to the church above by two passages to the north and south, which incorporate re-used Roman masonry. In Wilfrid's time, the main chamber may have served as a chapel and relic depository, lit by lamp niches. The eastern niche in the main chamber contains a late 14th-century alabaster panel from an altarpiece portraying the Resurrection. One of the niches in the north wall has been opened through into the passageway. According to tradition, if a young woman crawls through this opening, known as St Wilfrid's Needle, she will prove her virginity. Pass through the second chamber and follow the stairs up to the crossing.

MEDIEVAL WALLPAINTINGS

The interior of Roger's Church was decorated with lavish colour, traces of which can be seen in the eastern chapels of both transepts [10]. Beneath the gallery in the south transept is a room containing late 13th-century figurative paintings. This room is not generally accessible; if you wish to view the paintings, please ask. In one panel, a tonsured figure (perhaps a member of the Minster chapter) kneels in prayer before the Virgin and Child. In the next panel, the crowned Virgin stands holding a lily, a symbol of her purity. This area may, therefore, have been the original Lady Chapel.

THE CROSSING AND TRANSEPTS

It is in the crossing [11] that you can best appreciate the cruciform shape of the Cathedral. If you look up, you will see the Paschal Lamb, which conceals a trap door. The view of the crossing from here is spectacular (see p.5).
The transepts [12 and 13] are the best preserved element of Archbishop Roger's 12th-century Minster. Here can be seen the Transitional-style mixture of round-headed arches (used for details such as doors, windows, and the main arches supporting the crossing tower) and pointed arches (used for the decorative arcading).
When part of the 12th-century central tower collapsed in 1450, work began on rebuilding the crossing in the new Perpendicular style with pointed arches. As the work was never completed, Ripon possesses the unique feature of a central tower with two round and two pointed arches. The flat ceilings were introduced at that time.

The medieval pulpit.

Medieval wallpainting of the Virgin and Child.

The crossing from the central tower

The main chamber of Wilfrid's Crypt. [9]

✝HE PVLPI✝Vṃ

The 15th-century pulpitum divides the nave and the transepts from the choir and high altar, the more sacred parts of the church. Originally, a stone pulpit sat above, from which its name derives, and it was from here that the Gospel and Epistle were sung during Mass. The present pulpitum replaced an earlier screen, which was destroyed when the central tower collapsed in 1450. The original doors and image plinths bear the coats of arms of benefactors, including the Pigots of Clotherholme and the Wards of Givendale. Most of the statues were destroyed in the 16th or 17th centuries, the only element to survive being the Holy Trinity in the gable above the main doorway. The present statues in the niches date from 1947. They represent figures from the Cathedral's history, including St Willibrord (second from left), a pupil of St Wilfrid, who founded the monastery of Echternach in Luxemburg in 698.

THE ORGAN

The first 'great organ' was erected on the pulpitum loft in 1409. Payments to James Demssey in 1531 for work on the instrument suggest a re-build. This organ, perhaps destroyed during the Civil War, was replaced in 1695 by a new instrument by Gerard Smith. The present organ, with its case by Sir George Gilbert Scott, was first erected by T.C. Lewis in 1878 and was extended and rebuilt in 1912 by Harrison and Harrison.

Opposite the entrance to the Treasury is a statue of James I on a pedestal [15]. The statue, which dates from 1603, was made for the choir screen of York Minster, and was given to Ripon in the early 19th century.

Following in a long tradition of artistic patronage, the Cathedral continues to support modern artists. The lifesize sculpture of the Pieta, entitled 'Mother and Son', was made by Harold Gosney, in 1998 [16].

the south transept

In the gallery outside the Library are monuments to owners of the Studley Royal estate [17]. These include the Royalist, Sir John Mallorie (d. 1655), and John Aislabie (d. 1742), the Ripon MP (1695) and Chancellor of the Exchequer (1718). Aislabie was an investor in the South Sea Company, and when this enterprise collapsed in 1720 in the so-called South Sea Bubble, he was expelled from Parliament and barred thenceforth from public office. He retired to Studley and turned his hand to landscaping, creating the famous grounds and temples that still grace the estate adjoining Fountains Abbey.

On the south wall of the transept is a monument to William Weddell [18], an 18th-century owner of Newby Hall. Weddell, a member of the Dilettanti Society and a collector of Classical sculpture, erected a gallery at Newby to house the collection he brought back from his Grand Tour in 1765. His monument, 'a faint emblem of his refined taste', is, appropriately, a bust by Nollekens set beneath a classical rotunda. Below, in his epitaph by his widow he is described as possessing 'every virtue that enobles the mind'.

The effigy of Sir Thomas Markenfield [20]. His unusual collar portrays a stag imparked, probably a symbol of Henry IV.

The classical monument of William Weddell, an 18th-century owner of Newby Hall, near Ripon [18]. His impressive collection of sculpture can still be seen there.

THE NORTH TRANSEPT

During the Middle Ages, the north transept was the burial place of the Markenfields of nearby Markenfield Hall. Against the north wall is a tall tomb chest with the effigies of Sir Thomas Markenfield (d. 1497), a former sheriff of Yorkshire, and his wife [19]. The tomb of his grandparents lies between the two modern chapels [20]. The effigy of Lady Markenfield has been virtually effaced, but that of her husband, another Sir Thomas, is quite well preserved. He is shown in chainmail and plate armour. On the walls behind the modern altars are two 14th-century alabaster panels depicting the Coronation of the Virgin and a bishop, thought to be St Wilfrid. The original medieval pulpit [21], which used to stand on the pulpitum, now sits outside the entrance to the Treasury.

These two late-medieval gauntlets [22] probably formed part of the funeral achievements of the Markenfields and were originally hung over their tombs.

THE TREASURY

The Treasury contains both plate from diocesan churches and a number of items connected to the Cathedral.

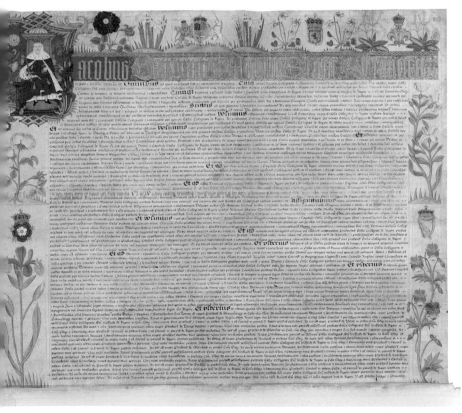

The Charter of James I [22], reconstituting the Chapter in 1604. King James is shown seated on his throne in the illuminated capital at the beginning of the document.

The Treasury.

THE CHANCEL

The chancel is divided into 2 distinct areas, each with its own liturgical function: the presbytery [23], with the High Altar, to the east, and the choir [24], with stalls for the clergy, to the west. The present chancel was shaped by Archbishop Roger; several of the western bays of the north arcade are from his time. The presbytery was reconstructed 100 years later in the Decorated style to house the shrines of St Wilfrid. The southern part of the choir was destroyed in 1450 with the collapse of the central tower. The reconstruction was paid for by the local gentry, including the Pigots of Clotherholme, whose coats of arms are above the stalls.

THE CHOIR

The daily Offices are held in the choir [24]. By the end of the Middle Ages the Minster was a large collegiate establishment with about 30 staff, almost all of which were to 'be present in the Quire...at matins, masse, evensonge and processions' daily. A large set of stalls were required to accommodate them. These were provided between 1489 and 1494 by William Bromflet's Ripon workshop.
Bromflet's stalls are tiered to reflect the occupant's rank. The higher stalls with towering canopies were for the use of the more senior clergy; the wider, more comfortable stalls along the western wall of the choir were for the use of the canons, with those further east reserved for the vicars choral. Below the main stalls is another row of seats for the lesser clergy and choristers

THE MISERICORDS

Each of the larger stalls has a tip-up seat with a misericord on its underside. Largely hidden, misericords gave ample scope to the imagination of the carver. Some have symbolic or moralistic forms, mythical animals, or angels holding shields. Bromflet was also inspired by printed sources. A number, including those depicting Jonah and the whale are derived from a German blockbook called the *Biblia Pauperum*.

The bench ends in the choir are elaborately carved. The bench end of the bishop's throne depicts an elephant carrying a castle full of people on its back.

On the mayor's stall, the 15th-century carver has attempted to portray a monkey.

The mechanical hand [25], installed in 1695, allowed the organist to direct the choir without leaving his seat in the loft.

Misericord [24] depicting Samson carrying away the gates of Gaza.

The choir [24]. The stalls are still used daily during Choral Evensong.

The Victorian ceiling of the chancel incorporates bosses from a 14th-century ceiling carved with biblical scenes. In this boss, the angel of the Lord expels Adam and Eve from the Garden of Eden.

THE HIGH ALTAR

The site of the present High Altar [26] in the Middle Ages was occupied by the most important of the two shrines of Saint Wilfrid (see p.24), whilst the medieval High Altar was west of the east wall. Some of its fittings remain, for example the 14th-century sedilia and a piscina [27]. The seats of the sedilia are placed under a pinnacled canopy. In the second set of pillars from the east are a number of iron hooks which in the Middle Ages probably supported a veil which concealed the High Altar during Lent.

The reredos [26] was designed in 1923 by Sir Ninian Comper as a memorial to the First World War. It is dominated by a large standing figure of the risen Christ, flanked by St Michael and St George. The reredos shows the Virgin and Child, surrounded by a series of Anglo-Saxon saints and historical figures. The corbels on either side of the High Altar support figures of the Cathedral's patrons: St Peter and St Wilfrid.

The east window contains glass of 1854 by Wailes of Newcastle, to commemorate the creation of the diocese of Ripon in 1836. Thought to be too bright, the window was altered in 1894 by A.O. Hemmings. The main composition is Christ commissioning the disciples.

The elaborately carved 14th-century sedilia [27] incorporates tiny crouching figures under the arches of its canopy.

The reredos [26], built as a war memorial, incorporates figures of Christ, saints, and also historical figures connected with Ripon.

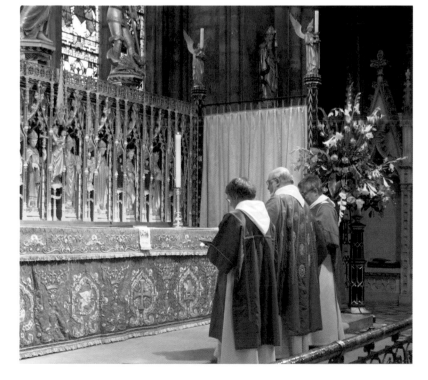

The High Altar [26] is used every Sunday for the Eucharist.

THE NORTH CHOIR AISLE

The eastern end of the north choir aisle [28] is screened off as the chapel of St Peter and has an altar formed out of the massive bowl of a font, probably from the time of Archbishop Roger.

The Chapel of the Resurrection.

The Chapter House.

THE SOUTH CHOIR AISLE

The east end of this aisle contains the Chapel of the Holy Spirit [29]. The gilded screens were designed by Leslie Durbin in the 1970s. The striking 'thunderbolt' effect is intended to evoke the descent of the Holy Spirit, in the form of tongues of fire, on the Apostles at Pentecost. The east window of the chapel has further glass by Wailes. The vivid colours of the figures of King David and Isaiah give some impression of the original appearance of the east window of the chancel.

The wall monument to Moses Fowler (d. 1608), last 'minister' of Ripon and first Dean of the James I foundation [30]. Although badly damaged during the Civil War, it shows him propped up on his shoulder. Above the monument is a tablet in memory of Robert Porteus, a native and member of the governing Legislature of Virginia when it was still a British colony. He died in Ripon in 1758.

The chapel of St Peter. It was re-dedicated in 1998, when the present altar (the font of the 12th-century Minster) was installed here.

The Chapel of the Holy Spirit.

THE CHAPTER HOUSE

The administrative heart of the Cathedral, the Chapter House [31], adjoins the south choir aisle. It functions as a vestry and working office and is not generally accessible to the public. During the Middle Ages, the room was divided in two. The eastern half served as a chapel, while the western half has probably always been used as a sacristy and for meetings of the governing Chapter. Its most distinctive architectural features are the two unusual circular windows in the south wall. The Chapel of the Resurrection is located in the vaulted undercroft beneath the Chapter House. Its altar is actually a section of column recovered from the foundations of the Anglo-Saxon Minster.

Near this Place
are deposited the Remains
of ROBERT PORTEUS ESQ.
a Native of Virginia & a Member of His Majesty's Council
or upper House of Legislature in that Province.
From thence he removed to England
and resided first at York, afterwards in this Town,
where he died August 8.1758.
Aged 79 Years.

THE CATHEDRAL LIBRARY

The Library [32] is approached by the oak staircase and gallery in the south transept. It was constructed above the Chapter House in the early 14th century. The north wall was originally the outside wall of Roger's choir. This gives you a chance to see the original 12th-century external windows and even some gargoyles. This chamber, known as the 'Lady Loft', may have replaced an earlier Lady Chapel in the south transept (see p.4) and was where masses for the Virgin were celebrated in the Middle Ages. To the right of the east window is a projecting corbel, to support a devotional image of the Virgin Mary.

Since the re-foundation of the Minster in the early 17th century, the Lady Loft has housed the working Chapter Library. The Library owns many rare books and manuscripts (now housed in the Brotherton Library at Leeds University for safe keeping) which came from the Library of Anthony Higgin, 2nd Dean of Ripon (1608-24). His badly-damaged monument can be seen on the south wall. Amongst the treasures owned by the Library are a Book of the Apocalypse (12th century), an illuminated English Bible (13th century), the Ripon Psalter (1418), a Flemish Book of Hours (15th century), an early printed edition of Boethius' *De Consolatione* by William Caxton (1490), and a copy of the 1549 *Book of Common Prayer*.

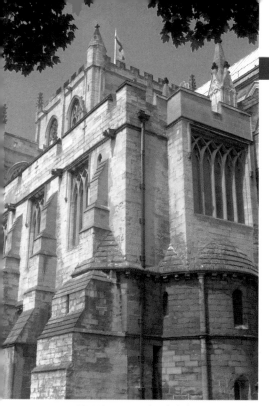

The 14th-century Lady Loft which now serves as the Cathedral Library [32].

16

St Wilfrid's Crypt.

Britain Around 660

When the first stones were laid at Ripon, England as we know it had not yet come into being. Instead, a patchwork of kingdoms stretched across Britain. Ripon lay within the huge northern kingdom of Northumbria (from the Humber to the Forth). At this time, Christianity was still not universally established in Britain. Pope Gregory I had sent Augustine as a missionary to Kent in 597. Three years later Paulinus was dispatched to Northumbria, where he began the construction of a cathedral at York. The conquest of Northumbria by the midland kingdom of Mercia in 633 led to the collapse of Christianity in the north. Fortunately, Northumbria was promptly liberated by King Oswald, who restored Christianity with the assistance of Aidan, an Irish monk from Iona who became bishop of Northumbria in 634. Unlike Paulinus, Aidan established his Episcopal headquarters on the island of Lindisfarne. The See of York was not restored until Wilfrid's consecration in 664.

Stephen of Ripon.

THE FOUNDATION OF RIPON MINSTER

The first monastery at Ripon was established around the year 657 by Eata, a Celtic monk from Melrose Abbey, on land granted by Alhfrith, son of King Oswiu of Northumbria and sub-king of Deira (modern Yorkshire). The Celtic monastery probably occupied an area north-east of today's Cathedral. In the following year, Alhfrith gave the monastery to Wilfrid, who relocated the church to its present site overlooking the River Skell. There he set about the construction of a Roman-style basilica of dressed stone with side-aisles and a crypt. The work was executed during the 660s and 670s and the new church was dedicated to St Peter. According to Stephen, a monk at Ripon and Wilfrid's biographer, the dedication ceremony was attended by Oswiu's successor, King Ecgfrith. The exact location of the other buildings remains uncertain. These were probably of timber and may have been sited north-east of the church, where the remains of a later Anglo-Saxon chapel, called the Ladykirk, and fragments of 8th or 9th-century stone crosses have also been discovered.

THE SYNOD OF WHITBY

The Synod of Whitby was convened by King Oswiu in 664 to resolve differences between the Irish (or Celtic) and Roman forms of Christianity. The conference addressed a number of controversies, including the correct dating of Easter. Celtic practices were defended by Bishop Colman of Northumbria and Abbess Hild of Whitby, while Roman customs were advocated by Agilbert, formerly bishop of the West Saxons, and Wilfrid. Oswiu found in favour of the Roman tradition and Colman, refusing to conform, withdrew to Iona. According to Bede, Tuda succeeded Colman but died of the plague shortly afterwards. Wilfrid was subsequently elected bishop of Northumbria in his place.

Fragments of 8th or 9th-century carved crosses.

THE LIFE OF ST. WILFRID

Wilfrid (b. 634) was the son of a Northumbrian aristocrat and one of the most influential and controversial figures of the 7th-century Church. Although initially educated by Celtic monks at Lindisfarne, he decided to embark upon the long and hazardous journey to Rome in 652. Afterwards, he spent three instrumental years at Lyons in the company of Bishop Aunemundus and became a monk. Once back in Northumbria, Wilfrid was granted the abbey at Ripon by Alhfrith in 658. Six years later, he acted as Bishop Agilbert's spokesman at the Synod of Whitby. His forthright defence of Roman customs led to their imposition throughout the Northumbrian Church. As a reward, Wilfrid travelled with Agilbert to Gaul, where he was consecrated Bishop of Northumbria.

He returned to discover that Chad had been intruded into his see. Wilfrid withdrew to Ripon but was restored to his bishopric by Archbishop Theodore of Canterbury in 669. Theodore's subsequent decision to subdivide the diocese of Northumbria in 678 prompted the first of two personal appeals to the Pope in Rome. Although successful, a series of further disputes meant that Wilfrid spent a total of 26 years of his episcopate in exile. During his enforced absences, he undertook missionary work in Sussex, served as bishop of Mercia, and established a chain of monasteries from Selsey to Hexham. Eventually, he agreed to retire and serve instead as bishop of Hexham. Wilfrid spent his last years at Ripon and died in 709. His body was buried south of the High Altar.

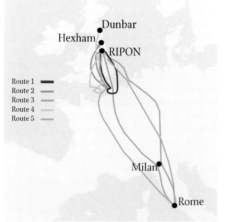

Route 1
Route 2
Route 3
Route 4
Route 5

Dunbar
Hexham
RIPON
Milan
Rome

Wilfrid's later journeys.

The Wilfrid window in the north transept by Harry Harvey (1977) depicts scenes from the saint's life.

WILFRID'S CHURCH

Other than Paulinus' Cathedral at York, the church constructed by Wilfrid at Ripon was probably the first stone building to have been built in northern England since the departure of the Romans in 410. In an age when kings lived in timber palaces, a stone church would have been an extraordinary sight. Contemporary accounts refer to the grandeur of Wilfrid's basilica. According to Stephen, the church was adorned with gold and silver and varied purples, while the High Altar was vested in purple woven with gold thread. Wilfrid also commissioned a set of illuminated gospels on purple parchment and a jewelled book-case. The Ripon Jewel is a rare example of such craftsmanship. Wilfrid's crypt also survives, built beneath the High Altar of Wilfrid's Church during the first century of English Christianity.

Construction of the crypt.

The 7th-century Ripon Jewel, displayed in the Treasury.

Reconstruction by Ivan Lapper of the Anglo-Saxon church at Jarrow.

Two of the ribs in the vault of the crypt's main chamber.

Panoramic view of the archaeological excavation in 1997.

The eastern niche probably housed relics brought from Rome. Other niches contained oil lamps to illuminate the chamber. Recent archaeological investigation by the York Archaeological Trust has revealed that the roof of the crypt was formed from stone ribs and mortar. This method of construction is otherwise unknown in England and its introduction at Ripon may well reflect Wilfrid's personal knowledge of Continental building practices. The passage roofs made use of recycled Roman masonry from Aldborough or York. The massive stone foundations of Wilfrid's Church were also uncovered. The picture which emerges is of a magnificent church, built with unusual materials and foreign techniques, at great cost and on an unprecedented scale.

KEY TO PANORAMA

1	Ribbed vault of western chamber
2	North wall of church
3	North passage - capstones for roof
4	Floor of Wilfrid's church
5	Ribbed vault of main chamber
6	South passage - capstones for roof
7	South wall of church
8	Victorian heating pipes

Seal of the medieval Chapter.

Seal of the medieval Commissary.

THE MIDDLE AGES

The Medieval Constitution

The Anglo-Saxon monastery at Ripon was probably converted into a college of secular canons shortly after the Norman Conquest. By 1230, there were seven canons attached to the Minster, each with his own living (or prebend) named after the principal village from which the canon derived his income. The canons of Stanwick, Monkton, Givendale, Studley, and Thorpe were provided with prebendal houses around the church, while the canon of Sharow resided in his parish. Together they formed the governing body or Chapter. Since there was no dean, the Prebendary of Stanwick enjoyed a degree of precedence as ruler of the choir. Similarly, the canon of Monkton always served as treasurer. Because pluralism and absenteeism were then rife amongst the clergy, each canon appointed a vicar to perform his duties. The vicars lived together in a purpose-built residence called the Bedern. They had their own common seal and elected a provost from their number. The church employed a staff of 31, including 6 vicars, 3 deacons, 6 sub-deacons, 6 thurifers and 6 choristers. Nine chantry chapels had also been founded by the Reformation to pray for the souls of their benefactors, and each was served by its own chaplain.

Thorpe Prebend House.

Common Seal of the vicars choral.

Ripon in the 14th century.

Ripon in the middle ages

The medieval archbishops of York maintained an episcopal palace and park at Ripon. In the 13th century the lordship became a liberty. Thereafter, the local authority of the sheriff was replaced by that of the archbishop, who enjoyed the privilege of appointing his own commission of the peace within the lordship. The liberty extended from the manor into the surrounding countryside, encompassing many neighbouring townships. However, the Chapter of Ripon Minster exercised their own independent authority within St Wilfrid's League. Their jurisdiction, which included the right of sanctuary, extended for approximately one mile in every direction from the Minster and was marked by eight mile-crosses located on the roads out of Ripon. The base of the Sharow Cross still survives. According to tradition, these rights were granted by King Athelstan in the 920s. The Chapter's privileges were later confirmed in the 12th century by King Stephen but jurisdictional disputes did still occur.

Local relations with the archbishops did not always remain cordial. Archbishop John Kemp's determination to exploit his secular rights led to violent outbursts during the 1440s. Angry tenants from the neighbouring lordship of Knaresborough destroyed the archbishop's park and mill in 1443. In response, Kemp recruited 300 soldiers from the Scottish border and fortified Ripon 'like a towne of warr'.

The Sharow Cross.

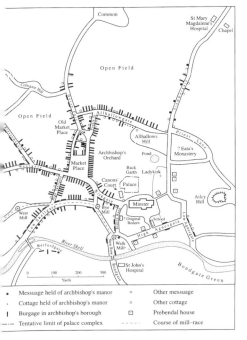

	Messuage held of archbishop's manor	○	Other messuage
•	Cottage held of archbishop's manor	▫	Other cottage
∣	Burgage in archbishop's borough	▫	Prebendal house
---	Tentative limit of palace complex	- - - -	Course of mill-race

12th-century indulgence for the rebuilding of the Minster.

ST WILFRID'S SHRINE

Ripon quickly became established as a centre of pilgrimage after Wilfrid's death. On the first anniversary a heavenly light is said to have illuminated the monastery. Such miraculous events began to attract large numbers of pilgrims. But Wilfrid's Church was burned by King Eadred of England in 948 in retaliation for the acceptance of Viking rule in Northumbria. How much damage was inflicted is unknown but the monastery survived since St Cuthbert's relics were brought here in 995. Sculpture, burials and coins of this period have all been found near the Cathedral.

St Mary Magdalene's Hospital.

According to one tradition, Archbishop Oda (942-959) removed Wilfrid's remains and took them back to Canterbury. Others insisted that Oda had mistakenly taken the remains of a later bishop. Archbishop Oswald of York (972-92) is said to have rediscovered the actual tomb in 979. The relics he found were reburied on the north side of the Minster.

Effigy of Walter de Gray in York Minster.

Construction commenced on a new Minster in the 12th century. Roger's Church was built to house the Shrine of St Wilfrid and its completion was marked by the translation of his relics in 1224. The body of the saint may have been reburied in the choir. The skull was encased in gold and enshrined separately, possibly behind the high altar. The Shrine continued to provide the Minster with a regular income throughout the Middle Ages. Ripon's medieval hospitals may have been founded to care for visiting pilgrims. St Wilfrid's Shrine was destroyed at the Reformation.

Artist's impression of the 12th-century Minster.

THE MEDIEVAL MINSTER

Ripon Cathedral is a testament to the wealth and patronage of the medieval archbishops of York. In the Middle Ages, the Minsters at Ripon, Beverley, and Southwell served as quasi-cathedrals within the archdiocese of York. The present building dates back to the 12th century. Its first known patron was Archbishop Roger de Pont l'Evêque (1154-81), who gave £1,000 to rebuild the Minster in the Transitional style. Roger commissioned his church at a time of great architectural change. The bolder features and rounded arches of the Norman (or Romanesque) style were being replaced by the lighter features and pointed arches of the Early English (or Gothic) style. Roger's new Minster was one of the earliest Gothic structures in England. The Chapter House, transepts, and crossing of Roger's Church still survive, together with fragments of the original aisleless nave.

Building continued throughout the Middle Ages. The west front was erected by Roger's successor, Walter de Gray (1215-56), in the early 13th century. With its triple portal and rank of lancet windows, it is the most striking part of the building, and has much in common with the north transept of York Minster, also the work of de Gray. In the 13th century, the eastern end of the choir was rebuilt in the Decorated style, probably during the archiepiscopates of John Romanus (1286-98), Henry Newark (1298-1300), and Thomas Corbridge (1300-1306). Construction of the Lady Chapel followed in the early 14th century. Much of the church was rebuilt in the Perpendicular style after the collapse of the central tower in 1450.

10th-century cross-head with a scene showing the mythological hero Sigurd sucking his burnt thumb after roasting a dragon's heart.

Edmer's Life of St Wilfrid provides historical information about the shrine.

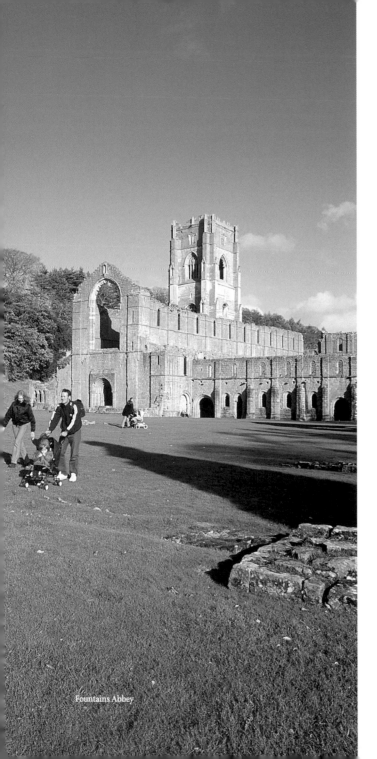

Fountains Abbey

FOUNTAINS ABBEY

In 1132, a small band of discontented Benedictine monks left St Mary's Abbey in York. They were dissatisfied with the worldliness of their house and sought a new life of greater austerity. They celebrated Christmas at Ripon as guests of Archbishop Thurstan (1114-41). On 27 December the monks travelled three miles west into Skelldale and founded Fountains Abbey on land given by the archbishop. They sheltered in caves and beneath an elm tree. In the following year, they were admitted into the Cistercian order and began construction of a timber monastery. The abbey flourished until its suppression by Henry VIII in 1539. The Cathedral continues to commemorate its historical link with an annual pilgrimage to Fountains on Boxing Day.

Medieval alabaster of St Wilfrid in the north transept.

The Boxing Day Pilgrimage.

A TROUBLESOME PRIEST

Marmaduke Bradley (d. 1553) was one of the most unscrupulous priests in the Minster's history. He was a Cistercian monk and a canon of Ripon. Having failed in his bid to become abbot of Fountains in 1536, Bradley resorted to bribery. Again unsuccessful, he turned his attention to Rievaulx Abbey. This time he offered Cardinal Wolsey his valuable prebend of Thorpe in return for his help. But his ambitions were thwarted. He then offered Thomas Cromwell his prebend and £200 for the abbacy of Fountains. Bradley was duly elected in 1536. Three years later, he surrendered his abbey to the king's commissioners in return for an annual pension of £100. But he refused to relinquish his prebend as agreed, and retired to Ripon a very wealthy man. In his last years, he served as residentiary canon and master of St Mary's Hospital.

REFORMATION AND RESTORATION

The Reformation

The English Reformation swept away all trace of the shrine of St Wilfrid. The college of canons survived the reign of Henry VIII only to be dissolved, along with the chantries, by Edward VI in 1547. The revenues of the Chapter were appropriated by the crown and Ripon Minster was reduced in status to a parish church served only by a handful of vicars. Catholic worship was briefly reintroduced during the reign of Mary Tudor and again when the rebel earls of Northumberland and Westmorland unfurled their standards at Ripon during the ill-fated Northern Rising of 1569.

14th-century alabaster panel of the Resurrection in the Crypt.

The Protestant regime found it rather more difficult to stamp out Catholic sympathies within the hearts of the local population. A number of Elizabethan priests were accused of refusing to comply with the new regulations for public worship or concealing proscribed images, books and altars within the church. Instructions were also given to block up St Wilfrid's Needle and destroy the altar in the crypt, which had survived against all odds.

Ripon Cathedral's fine collection of medieval alabaster tablets was carefully hidden by devoted Catholics around this time. They were rediscovered beneath the dean's stall in the choir during the 19th century.

RECONSTITUTION

In 1604, the Chapter was re-established by James I at the behest of Queen Anne of Denmark. One of the former vicars, Moses Fowler, became the first dean. He was joined by six prebendaries, although these were now numbered by choir stall (or seat). Three years later, the privileges of the Chapter were augmented and a sub-dean instituted.

The Chapter in 1999 with Bishop Ralph Emmerson, on the 60th anniversary of his ordination.

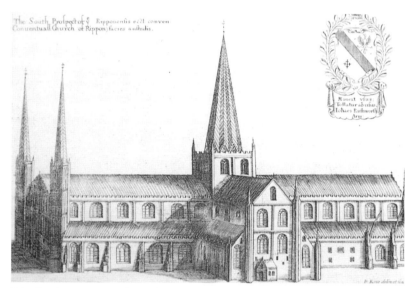

This early 17th-century engraving by Daniel King shows the Cathedral before the loss of the spires.

THE CIVIL WAR

Ripon was occupied by Parliamentarian troops during the English Civil War. Soldiers under the command of Sir Thomas Mauleverer destroyed much of the medieval stained glass, including the magnificent great east window. Many monuments were also defaced. The chapter was once again disbanded during the Commonwealth (1649-1660) but revived by Charles II after the Restoration of 1660. In the same year, the great central spire fell through the roof into the choir, causing serious damage to Bromflet's stalls. The cost of repairing the damage was estimated to have been £6,000, and the spire was never rebuilt. In 1664, the twin western spires were dismantled as a precaution.

Bishop Charles Longley.

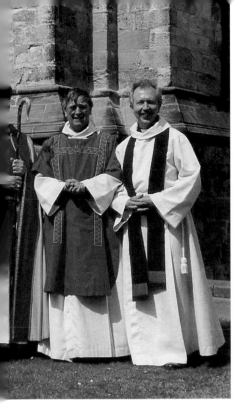

THE MODERN CATHEDRAL

A New Beginning

The modern diocese of Ripon was created in 1836. Ripon Minster became the Cathedral Church of the first new English diocese to be founded since the Reformation. The Chapter was reduced in size to a dean and four residentiary canons. The first bishop of the new diocese was Charles Thomas Longley. After centuries of neglect, the fabric of the Cathedral was in desperate need of repair. Major restoration work was carried out during the 1860s under the direction of Sir George Gilbert Scott (1811-78), a leading figure in the Gothic Revival. Much of the Cathedral was re-roofed, and the central tower and west front strengthened. The total cost was £40,000. The duty of restoration and preservation for future generations continues to this day.

The diocese was renamed the diocese of Ripon and Leeds in 2000. New Cathedral Statutes were instituted in September 2001. Today, the Chapter comprises a dean and 2 residentiary canons, a chapter clerk, 3 lay persons and a representative of the diocese.

Restoration of the west front was completed in 2002.

Portrait of James I from the Cathedral Collection.

The Old Hall.

The rabbit hole misericord.

FAMOUS FACES

Lewis Carroll

Charles Lutwidge Dodgson (1832-98) was more commonly known as Lewis Carroll, the author of Alice's Adventures in Wonderland. His father became a residentiary canon of the Cathedral in 1852. During his many visits to Ripon, Carroll wrote *Ye Carpette Knyghte* and several pages of *Through the Looking-Glass*, as well as a number of mathematical papers. Many were written at the Old Hall in High St Agnesgate, where the family was accommodated when Canon Dodgson was in residence. Carroll's work may have been inspired by carvings in the choir, especially the misericord of a griffin chasing a rabbit down a rabbit hole. Sir George Gilbert Scott depicted the Queen of Hearts and the Cheshire Cat in the south transept to commemorate this connection. Canon Dodgson is commemorated on the clergy board beneath the south-west tower.

Lewis Carroll.

Wilfred Owen

Wilfred Owen (1893-1918) was perhaps the finest English poet of the First World War. He served on the Somme before being sent home in 1917 suffering from shell-shock. After a period of convalescence in Scotland, he returned to light regimental duties. In March 1918, he was posted to the Northern Command Depot at Ripon. A number of poems were composed in Ripon, including 'Futility' and 'Strange Meeting'. His 25th birthday was spent quietly in the Cathedral. Owen rejoined his battalion at Amiens in September 1918, and was immediately awarded the Military Cross for gallantry. He was killed in the early morning of 4 November, during the last week of the war.

Wilfred Owen.

THE CATHEDRAL TODAY

The Mother Church of the Diocese of Ripon and Leeds today maintains its tradition of the finest worship and cathedral music. You have joined the many visitors and pilgrims who are welcomed to the Cathedral every day of the year. As a living Church, we maintain a pastoral ministry in our parish and play host to many special events each year, including the great Christian festivals of Easter, Christmas, and most especially for Ripon, the Feast of Candlemas. This takes place every February when the Cathedral blazes with thousands of candles as we remember the Holy Family presenting Christ in the Temple. We try to maintain our work by supporting a Development Campaign which provides funds for our ministry, music, and educational projects. Our choral music is amongst the finest in the country, our concerts and art events vital to the cultural life of North Yorkshire. The Bishop, whose seat or cathedra is found here, teaches his Diocese and ordains and trains his clergy where the Faith has been proclaimed for over 1300 years. We celebrate our rich inheritance of faith and history, and strive to live as Jesus would have us live, as a Pilgrim people of God.

Candlemas.

The Millennium Service.

A mason at work.

GLOSSARY

Arcade   A series of arches.

Basilica   A rectangular church with a nave, side aisles and an eastern apse.

Chapter House   The room in which the Chapter, or governing body, meets.

Choir   The western half of the eastern arm of a great church, containing choir stalls where the daily Offices are sung.

Clerestory   A series of windows which light the upper storeys of a church.

Corbel   A projecting stone which supports a statue or an arch.

Crossing   The point where the choir, nave, and transepts intersect. The crossing is usually surmounted by a central tower.

Decorated style   The style prevalent in the later 13th and early 14th century, characterised by elaborate geometric and flowing forms in window design and decorative foliage.

High Altar   The principal altar of the church.

Minster   A large collegiate church.

Misericord   A ledge on the underside of a hinged seat in a choir stall which, when turned up, supports the person standing in the stall.

Nave   The western part of a church, reserved for use by the laity.

Perpendicular style   The latest form of Gothic architecture prevalent from about 1400, characterised by large windows with vertical forms and elaborate panelled decoration.

Piscina   A basin used for washing the chalice and paten after Communion.

Presbytery   The eastern part or sanctuary of the church, containing the High Altar

Pulpitum   The stone screen between the crossing and choir. Its name derives from the pulpit which used to sit on top of it.

Reredos   An altarpiece.

Sedilia   Group of three seats in the sanctuary occupied by the principal clergy during Communion.

Stall   One of the enclosed seats for either choir or clergy.

Transepts   The north and south arms of a cruciform church.

Transitional style   The architectural style prevalent at the end of the 12th century and containing elements from the earlier Norman style (with round arches) and the new Early English Gothic style (with pointed arches).